The Man Behind the Gun

Samuel Colt and His Revolver

Edwin Brit Wyckoff

Enslow Elementary
an imprint of
Enslow Publishers, Inc.
40 Industrial Road
Box 398
Berkeley Heights, NJ 07922
USA

http://www.enslow.com

Content Adviser
Kurt House, M.A.
Director, Colt Collectors Association

Series Literacy Consultant
Alan A. De Fina, Ph.D.
Past President, New Jersey Reading Association
Chairperson, Department of Literacy Education,
New Jersey City University

Enslow Elementary, an imprint of Enslow Publishers, Inc.

Enslow Elementary® is a registered trademark of Enslow Publishers, Inc.

Library of Congress Cataloging-in-Publication Data

Wyckoff, Edwin Brit.
  The man behind the gun : Samuel Colt and his revolver / Edwin Brit Wyckoff.
     p. cm. — (Genius at work! Great inventor biographies)
  Includes bibliographical references and index.
  Summary: "Readers will learn about Samuel Colt, the revolver, and mass production"—Provided by publisher.
  ISBN 978-0-7660-3446-4
  1. Colt, Samuel, 1814-1862—Biography—Juvenile literature. 2. Gunsmiths—United States—Biography—
Juvenile literature. 3. Colt revolver—History—Juvenile literature. I. Title.
  TS533.62.C65W935 2010
  683.40092—dc22
  [B]

                           2009028129

Printed in the United States of America

042010 Lake Book Manufacturing, Inc., Melrose Park, IL

10 9 8 7 6 5 4 3 2 1

Contents

Before Colt's invention of the revolver, guns were slow to load and hard to use.

Chapter 1

The Jackknife That Carved an Empire

Way, way back in the late 1800s, there rarely was such a thing as a fair fight even if you had a pistol or rifle. A gang of armed men could easily surround a lawman whose gun carried only one bullet at a time. Or a rebellious crew on a sailing ship could corner the captain and first mate. The captain had all the guns, but he had too many targets crowding in on him.

Think back to the Wild West, where a settler with only one bullet in his gun tried to outrun an American Indian warrior. The Indian stopped short, reached over his shoulder to pull out one arrow, and sent it flying. He followed it with another and another. Indian warriors could fire off their arrows faster than a settler could reload. And the Indian had a quiver full of arrows. The settler did not want to waste a bullet unless he would hit his target. He might not get a chance to reload, aim, and fire a second shot.

The world had to wait for Samuel Colt and his invention. It was a handgun that could fire off six bullets before it had to be reloaded. Colt thought he could change the odds so that one man could fight off half a dozen.

Samuel Colt was born on July 19, 1814, to Christopher and Sarah Colt, near Hartford, Connecticut. His adoring mother died when he was seven years old. His stepmother, Olivia, sent Sam and his brothers and sisters to live and work in other people's homes. After about a year, his father called Sam home to work in his factory. Sam's father believed in work first and schooling second. Although the boy was a poor student, he learned to read and loved it. But he never learned to spell very well.

Samuel Colt

When Sam was fourteen years old, he attended Amherst Academy. But he was just not interested in following the rules of the school. He often was in trouble, especially when he brought a pistol to school and fired it off. Rather than risk getting expelled, Sam left the school.

According to one story, a short while after this incident, Sam announced that he would blow up a raft in the middle of the lake in Ware, Connecticut. On July 4, 1829, everyone dressed up and marched out to watch the fun on the lake. Young Sam Colt made a deep bow to the audience. Then he set off a powerful explosion under the raft. The air filled with a shower of muddy water that rained down on the watchers below. The wet, wild, angry crowd chased Sam, wanting to tear him apart with their own muddy hands.

Sam slipped away safely, thanks to Elisha Root, who had been watching. Root was impressed that Sam had been able to send an electric charge underwater. Sam had simply wrapped the line in tarred cloth, giving it a waterproof seal.

Eager to get out of town, Sam went to sea. In 1830, Sam got a job on a sailing ship, the *Corvo*. The teenager traveled thousands of miles to places like Calcutta and London.

A sailing ship like those used in the 1830s

Colt used his jackknife to carve a model of his revolving pistol. Above are a ship's wheel (on left) and a capstan. These may have given Colt his idea.

At night, Sam would sit alone on deck in the blue-white light from the moon. He held a cheap jackknife in his fist and carved a block of wood into a strange-  looking gun. It had a revolving cylinder with six little tubes holding one bullet each. The cylinder could spin around so that bullets could be fired one after another. Colt may have gotten the idea for the revolving cylinder while watching the spin of the wheel that steered the ship or the turning of the capstan that raised the anchor.

Colt was not making a toy. He was inventing his whole future.

Chapter 2

Dr. Coult and His Laughing Gas

One dark night, the *Corvo* slipped back into an American harbor. Sam was tired of life on the sea. The world traveler went home to work in his father's factory. He learned how to bleach cloth and color it with dyes. He handled tools, mixed chemicals, and learned how to keep all sorts of machines up and running.

But Sam was not happy. He began to feel that his whole life was being swallowed up by the roaring, rattling machines. In 1931, he broke loose again. Sam wanted to start making his revolver. But he could not do that without lots of money. He came up with a very unusual idea about how to raise the money.

By now, Sam Colt was a tall, good-looking young man. He decided to reinvent himself as "Dr.

Coult," the mysterious scientist. He would pretend to give scientific lectures. He pumped laughing gas into masks on the faces of volunteers. The gas was nitrous oxide, used by dentists to keep patients pain-free while their teeth were being drilled. The gas also made them giggle and hop around. Sam pumped in just enough gas to keep his volunteers laughing and jumping. The crowd roared with laughter. The show was a terrific money-maker.

Soon after, young Dr. Coult changed his name back to Sam Colt and started pouring his profits into that strange gun he had invented. He hired experts to turn his hand-carved wooden gun into a handmade steel gun that could fire six bullets without having to be reloaded. In 1832, the eighteen-year-old inventor applied for a U.S. patent to protect his design. The patent was awarded in 1835, and he was ready to take on the world.

Genius at Work!

1. The trigger lever pushes the hammer back.

2. The hammer presses against a spring in the gun's handle.

3. The cylinder rotates so that the next chamber is in front of the barrel.

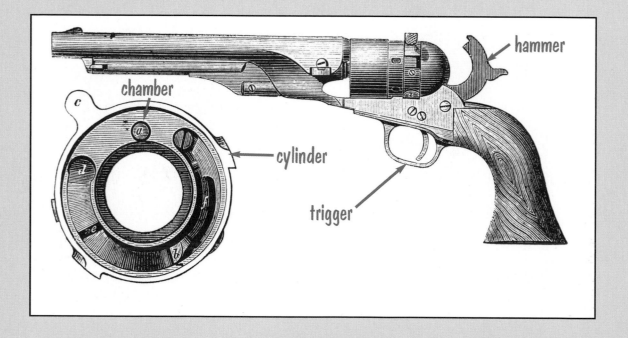

Chapter 3

Colt Sells His Six-Shooter

Samuel Colt took a giant step into an American age of invention. Sailing ships were being outraced by steamboats. Wagon trains were losing business to railroads. Colt's friend, Samuel F. B. Morse, created a successful telegraph. He also invented Morse code.

Samuel F. B. Morse, a friend of Colt's, was the inventor of the telegraph. In this painting, he is sending a telegram using Morse code.

Messages could be sent across wires using the code's dots and dashes. People could tap out messages at blinding speed. Samuel Colt wanted to be part of that new world of invention.

With an uncommon level of courage, Colt started a factory in 1836 in Paterson, New Jersey. He used the money he had raised from his performances as Dr. Coult. He also got some money from his father and other investors excited by the idea of a gun that could change the odds in war and in peacekeeping.

Colt had each of the designs for his revolvers tested by lawmen such as the Texas Rangers before a final design was approved. Each part of the gun was cut from steel. Wooden handles and decorations

were added. And each gun was polished till it shone.

It was time to sell his six-shooters. All Colt needed was one large order to launch his business. He even tried to persuade President Andrew Jackson that fast-firing repeaters would give his soldiers a winning edge. Before he was president, Jackson had been the general who won the Battle of New Orleans in the War

President Andrew Jackson

of 1812. Colt was sure the old general would understand the extraordinary firepower of a six-shooter. But Jackson was not convinced. Sam Colt's bid for a U.S. Army contract was turned down flat.

By now, Colt was getting desperately short of cash. He managed to stay just one step ahead of the bill collectors as he failed to win contract after contract from the government. He made exciting sales pitches to get money from investors. He also held fancy dinner parties to attract a bigger circle of investors. Nothing worked.

Unable to get a government contract for his revolvers, Colt turned to another project: a harbor defense system. He wanted to use underwater bombs to protect harbors from invading ships. To design the system, Colt reached back to his teenage experience in blowing up the raft. He wrapped electrical wires in tar-soaked fabric. The waterproof lines could run underwater and trigger bombs from a safe distance. But Colt could not find a single customer or even one investor ready to put up money.

Every time Colt tried selling his guns to the U.S. Army, he found that every military warehouse and fort was stuffed with cannonballs. But there was never any money for revolvers and repeating rifles. Military officers and lawmen were begging for Colt's six-shooters. Strangely, two stubborn Army colonels,

Colt might have had more luck selling his six-shooter to the Army if George Talcott had not owned a factory that made cannonballs.

George Bombord and George Talcott, turned Colt down again and again.

The secret behind this story is that Talcott owned an iron foundry in Richmond, Virginia, that poured out most of those cannonballs, making huge profits for Talcott.

When the secret was discovered, Talcott was dismissed from the U.S. Army. Colt moved in fast and landed his first big military contract in 1846. The U.S. Army ordered a thousand revolving pistols. There was just one problem: By this time, Colt no longer had a factory to make them.

Chapter 4

Mass Production Makes Masses of Money

Gun makers had always built guns by hand, one at a time. Sam Colt wanted to make each part by the thousands. Then he would have each gun put together like a puzzle. Every barrel, cylinder, handle, and all the other parts were made exactly the same by machine. It was like a giant Lego set with piles of thousands of interchangeable pieces. Any piece could be used instead of another. An assembly line of workers put the pieces together by hand. Each worker assembled one portion of the gun and then passed it along to another worker, who assembled another portion. This was repeated until they had a finished, working revolver.

This process is called mass production. Mass production is faster, cheaper, and more profitable than crafting each item by hand. Almost everything from cars to computers is mass-produced today.

Colt had been forced to shut down his Patterson factory in about 1841. He had not gotten enough orders to keep the factory going. So when he

Mass production is used for all kinds of manufacturing. Here, assembly-line workers in Illinois make washing machines in 1945, like Colt's factory made revolvers.

finally won a large military contract in 1846, Colt had to hire another factory to produce his guns.

With the profits from this order, Colt was able to open a factory of his own in 1847. He got more contracts from the U.S. military for his revolvers.

The Colt Peacemaker

Over the years, Colt designed a variety of revolvers. His Peacemaker revolver was especially popular in the American West. The Navy Colt was a popular model among U.S. navy officers. And the Dragoon was one of Colt's best sellers.

The Colt Navy revolver

Other countries began buying the fast-firing weapons as well. In 1851, Colt packed up his guns and took them overseas, demonstrating them in Russia, England, Turkey, and France. Colt gave lectures on mass production, and the world applauded him by buying the weapons in huge numbers.

In 1855, Colt built a huge new factory in Hartford, Connecticut. It was 60 feet wide and 500

COLT'S PATENT FIRE ARMS MANUFACTORY,
HARTFORD CONN

Colt built a huge factory in Hartford, Connecticut, to manufacture his revolvers.

feet long. Five hundred people worked at hundreds of machines powered by steam engines.

Colt's high level of production came at the same time as a surge in demand. In the United States, the North and the South were at odds. The southern states were threatening to break away from the United States and form their own country. It seemed that war was not far off. Both the North and the South were stocking up on military firepower. Neither side could risk being outgunned.

Chapter 5

Mass-Producing a Whole New World

Samuel Colt insisted that he would not be second in anything. That was his lifetime goal. He had ideas, money, an amazing personality, and endless energy. He had the power to build a new world.

Always racing and running, investing and inventing, Colt had not had time to find a wife when he was a young man. On June 5, 1856, when he was forty-two, he married Elizabeth Jarvis. To celebrate, they traveled the world. On their honeymoon, they even attended the ceremony when Alexander II was crowed czar of Russia.

Sam and Elizabeth Colt had four children. Sadly, only one of them, Caldwell Colt, lived past childhood. Sam Colt's workers seemed to become his family.

The home Colt built for his family

He built them parks, fountains, gardens, and a museum. Everyone loved the sound of his giant factory whistle, which could be heard twenty miles up and down the Connecticut valleys.

Colt built a whole new town with houses for families, boardinghouses for single people, and a meeting hall that could hold every one of his workers. He made plans to set up a technical college to train people so they could learn new skills and earn better wages. Unfortunately, the school never opened.

In 1861, the American Civil War exploded, pitting the North against the South. Colt's output of guns was staggering. During the war, the factory mass-produced 7,000 rifles, 113,000 muskets, and an astonishing 387,000 six-shooters. The man who always had more talk than cash began making millions of dollars—and spending them as more and more millions poured in.

Colt was forty-five years old in 1861 when the Civil War began. The war made him unbelievably

A painting of the Battle of Gettysburg in the Civil War

rich. He had climbed a mountain of money and fame that seemed to go on forever.

Without warning, a simple chest cold Colt had caught became a serious fever. Colt developed pneumonia. All the money he had could not make him well. On January 10, 1862, Samuel Colt died. He left a fortune equal to $200 million today. He was only forty-seven years old. His guns had won wars. His Peacemaker six-shooters had won the West. His inventions and his ideas about mass production had changed the way the world worked.

The teenage sailor with a jackknife in his fist had carved his name into the history of war-making and peacekeeping forever.

Timeline

1814 Samuel Colt is born July 19, on family farm near Hartford, Connecticut.

1829 Blows up raft on lake in Ware, Connecticut, during July Fourth celebration.

1830 Goes to sea on sailing ship *Corvo* on August 2. Carves wooden revolver.

1831 Appears as the mysterious Dr. Coult, giving scientific lectures and drugging volunteers with laughing gas.

1832 Applies for United States patent to protect six-shooter design.

1836 Awarded patent on December 3. Demonstrates six-shooter for President Andrew Jackson.

1855 Builds huge new factory near Hartford, Connecticut; installs assembly line and mass-production system.

1856 Marries Elizabeth Jarvis.

1862 Dies January 10.

Words to Know

assembly line—An arrangement in which products are made step by step as they pass along a line of machines and workers.

contract—An agreement to supply a product or do work at a certain price and at a certain time.

czar (ZAR)—The ruler of Russia before 1917.

investor—Someone who puts money into a business, hoping to earn money in return.

musket—A gun with a long barrel; used in warfare before modern rifles were invented.

nitrous oxide—Also known as "laughing gas"; a gas that is inhaled to reduce pain.

pistol—A small gun that is held and fired with one hand.

profit—Money earned when doing business or selling something.

revolver—A pistol with a revolving cylinder that holds bullets. It can be fired several times without reloading.

rifle—A long gun that is fired from the shoulder. A repeating rifle can be fired several times without reloading.

six-shooter—A revolver that holds six bullets.

Books

Byam, Michele. *Arms & Armor.* New York: DK Children, 2004.

Clements, Gillian. *The Picture History of Great Inventors.* London: Frances Lincoln Children's Books, 2005.

Gifford, Clive. *1000 Years of Famous People.* New York: Kingfisher Publications, 2002.

Murdoch, David S. *Eyewitness: Cowboy.* New York: DK Children, 2000.

Internet Addresses

Colt History
http://colt.com/mil/history.asp

Samuel Colt: Inventor
http://www.infoplease.com/biography/var/samuelcolt.html

Samuel Colt: Who Made America?
http://www.pbs.org/wgbh/theymadeamerica/whomade/colt_hi.html

Index